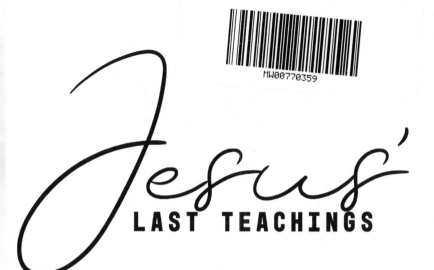

Jesus'

LAST TEACHINGS

PROPERTY OF:

_____

MW00770359

LAST TEACHINGS

Published by

Life Bible Study, LLC is a Christian Publisher serving churches and Christian communities in order to advance the Gospel of Jesus Christ, making disciples as we go.

© 2018 Life Bible Study

All rights reserved. No part of this publication may be reproduced, stored in a retrieval system, or transmitted in any form or by any means, electronic, mechanical, photocopying, recording, or otherwise, without the prior permission of Life Bible Study. Address all correspondence to:

Life Bible Study, LLC
5184 Caldwell Mill Road
Suite 204-221
Hoover, AL 35244

Unless otherwise indicated, all Scripture quotations are from the ESV® Bible (The Holy Bible, English Standard Version®), copyright © 2001 by Crossway, a publishing ministry of Good News Publishers. Used by permission. All rights reserved.

ISBN Number 978-1-63204-072-5

31 Verses Every Believer Should KnowTM

www.lifebiblestudystore.com
www.31verses.com

Printed in the United States of America

INTRODUCTION

As Jesus led His disciples during His last week in Jerusalem, He taught them along the journey. And He continued teaching throughout the week. He taught through delivering prophecy, through allowing people to see His emotions on display, through His actions that took on the role of living parables, through His responses to conflict and criticism, and through the way He completed His mission on earth. His audiences varied, and included His disciples and His followers, the crowds in Jerusalem, the religious leaders, the merchants in the Temple court, the political powers in Judah, and even the Roman soldiers. Everyone who encountered Jesus during this week had the opportunity to see or hear Him teach.

Studying Jesus' teachings during this final week is like taking a master's course in teaching methodology, in understanding the audience, in passionately conveying the content, and of living out, fully committed, what is taught. Jesus taught from His authority as the Son of God and out of His deep love and compassion for mankind. Jesus passionately wanted to bring all people back to God, and He agonized when some of His audience rejected His message. Even facing the humiliation and pain of the cross did not change His message.

Jesus provides us with the opportunity to see the supreme Teacher in action. Not only can we be changed during the process, but we might even become passionate about how we, too, teach with our words, actions, and lives.

Jesus' last week is often referred to as the Passion Week. That title captures the energy of the week, the emotional ups and downs of dealing with people who didn't get who God is and what Jesus was sent to do, the pain and sorrow experienced on the cross, and the joy of His resurrection.

So, if you're ready, let's start the journey.

Margie Williamson
Editor

HOW TO USE

31 Verses Every Believer Should Know: **Jesus' Last Teachings—A Lenten Study**

How can you get the most out of this study for Lent?

Consider these suggestions . . .

1. Read the devotions provided for each week of Lent. Daily Bible study and personal reflection can give you the opportunity to mourn over Jesus' suffering and celebrate His resurrection.

2. Memorize the verse included with each devotion.

3. Respond to the questions that accompany the devotions either in writing or mentally.

4. Pray daily that God will allow this journey to teach you something new about Jesus, so that you might renew your commitment to Him.

Jesus

LAST TEACHINGS

PROCLAIMING HIS COMING DEATH

"See, we are going up to Jerusalem. And the Son of Man will be delivered over to the chief priests and scribes, and they will condemn him to death."
—Matthew 20:18

When was the last time someone started to tell you something with the words, "Well, I have good news and bad news. Which do you want to hear first?" Did your heart start racing when you heard those words? Were your hands shaky or sweaty? Or did you simply think the person was just being dramatic to get your attention? If you were indeed going to receive both good news and bad news, which would you prefer to hear first? How difficult is it to focus on the good news, especially if you've already heard the bad news?

Read Matthew 20:17-19. Jesus had twice predicted His coming death to His disciples (see Mt. 16:23 and 17:22-23). In both instances, despite having witnessed Christ's true identity, the disciples were distressed by what would happen to Him. In chapter 20, as Jesus led His disciples up to Jerusalem for the last time, He reminded them that He would be delivered to the chief priests and scribes, who would condemn Him to death, and hand Him over to the Roman authorities to crucify Him. This time, however, Jesus promised that He would be raised from the dead on the third day. Yet once again, the disciples couldn't hear the good news of His resurrection because they were so focused on the bad news of His death.

Jesus knew that His mission as Messiah would lead Him to the cross, and He also knew that He would be resurrected from the dead. His full awareness of God's plan along with His complete trust in His Father allowed Him to endure the bad news for the joy that would be found when the good news came true.

When we hear "good news and bad news," we tend to focus on the bad news and overlook the good news. Jesus' emphasis, however, was on the good news of what He would do for all mankind, not on the bad news of what He would experience.

How were Jesus' predictions of His death and resurrection both bad news and good news?

Why do you think the disciples heard Jesus would suffer, but couldn't hear that He would be raised to life?

How does Jesus' completed work as our Messiah give us joy and hope?

PROCLAIMING HIS COMING DEATH

"Now is my soul troubled. And what shall I say? 'Father, save me from this hour'? But for this purpose I have come to this hour."—John 12:27

Receiving news of a life-threatening illness is never easy. Most people have to work through the stages of grief, which according to Elizabeth Kübler-Ross' classic book *On Death and Dying*, include denial, anger, bargaining, depression, and acceptance. Even with time and work, some people are never able to accept their own mortality and impending death.

Read John 12:23-28. In John 12:12-19, Jesus entered Jerusalem riding a donkey, visually announcing to all who saw Him that He was the Son of God who had come to sacrifice His life for others. Yet, verses 23-28 show the human struggle Jesus faced as He questioned what He had come to do. In verse 27, He wondered if He could ask God to save Him from what He would have to endure. These words remind us of His time in the garden of Gethsemane (see Mt. 26:36-46). *The Expositor's Bible Commentary* stated that Jesus "shrank from a death that was imposed unjustly, executed cruelly, and could brand Him as a rebel and a criminal." In the garden, Jesus came to the same conclusion that He had come to in these verses—His death was necessary to provide a way for people to be redeemed and restored to God.

In His last week on earth, Jesus demonstrated both His humanity and His divinity. He experienced the grief of knowing that His time was coming to an end, and He was saddened by the relationships that would change. Yet, His divinity led Him to the understanding that what He had come to do was necessary. Although He must have struggled with these questions until His arrest, He recognized that what He had come to do would open the way for people to be restored to God. In the end, Jesus accepted His role in God's plan for us.

What does it mean to you to grieve? Have you experienced grief that was almost more than you could handle? Record those feelings.

How did you manage to move beyond your personal grief?

How does knowing that Jesus struggled to accept God's call on His life help you accept God's call on your life?

PROCLAIMING HIS COMING DEATH

"And I, when I am lifted up from the earth, will draw all people to myself."
—John 12:32

Most Protestant churches display empty crosses in their sanctuaries, while Catholic churches display the crucifix—the image of the cross upon which the body of Jesus hangs. Why this difference? Protestants tend to focus on the empty cross because it signifies that Jesus is risen from the dead and is no longer there. Catholics cite the crucifix as a reminder that Jesus' ministry and purpose was to die upon the cross. Archbishop Fulton Sheen explained the use of the crucifix with these words: "Keep your eyes on the crucifix, for Jesus without the cross is a man without a mission, and the cross without Jesus is a burden without a reliever."[1]

Read John 12:29-33. John recorded these words to make sure his readers understood the kind of death Jesus would suffer. It would not be an easy death or a quick death or a painless death. Instead, Jesus would be executed through crucifixion, with His hands and feet painfully nailed to the wooden cross, after which the bottom end of the cross would be placed in a hole so Jesus would hang above the crowds. Yet, despite the pain and the humiliation, John emphasized that Jesus did what He did to give all people the opportunity for salvation. Not only would Jesus be lifted up in the process of crucifixion, but He would lift up all those who accepted His salvation to restore them to God.

Protestants and Catholics tend to argue theological tenets, such as the empty cross versus the crucifix. Both are important. Both remind us of Jesus' work of salvation on the cross. Both point to the resurrection, the empty cross from the other side, and the crucifix from before it happened. The question is not which is better, but how we respond to both.

---

[1] Patrick Madrid, "Why do Catholics have crucifixes?" Available on-line at https://www. thebostonpilot.com/article.asp?ID=6018.

Which cross helps you most clearly understand what Jesus has done for you—the empty cross or the crucifix? Why?

How do you see Jesus lifted up in your life? Why?

Why do you think so many people refuse to accept Jesus' offer of salvation?

PROCLAIMING HIS COMING DEATH

Therefore he had to be made like his brothers in every respect, so that he might become a merciful and faithful high priest in the service of God, to make propitiation for the sins of the people.—Hebrews 2:17

In the movie *Star Trek: The Wrath of Khan*, Spock was inside a radioactive chamber and knew that he was going to die. Through a glass wall, he said to his friend and commander, "It is logical. The needs of the many outweigh the needs of the few." Commander Kirk responded, "Or the one. . ."[1] In a series that told the story of the crew of the *USS Enterprise* who traveled the galaxy to protect the needs of the many, Spock's and Kirk's words represented an on-going theme.

Read Hebrews 2:14-18. The writer of Hebrews told the story of the Son of God who came to earth as a human with one purpose—to give His own life for the many. By conquering death, He opened the way for us to have eternal life, overcame evil by destroying Satan and freeing us from his grip, and restored the many back into the presence of God. To do this, Jesus had to become human, to "share in flesh and blood" with God's children (v. 14) so He would "be fit for the task" as the faithful high priest.[2] The writer used the word *propitiation*, which scholar Charles Ryrie defined as "the turning away of wrath by an offering,"[3] to describe this act. Propitiation produces two outcomes: turning God's anger away from us as sinners, and restoring us back into God's presence. Both outcomes would be accomplished through Jesus' death and resurrection.[4]

Trekkies and non-Trekkies have debated Spock's statement throughout the years. Some have questioned whether it is truly logical to put the needs of another first. Yet while others argue over the logic, Jesus demonstrated His willingness to die for us, to put our needs first, to bring us back into the presence of God.

---

[1] Quoted at http://www.imdb.com/title/tt0084726/quotes.
[2] Edgar V. McKnight & Christopher Church, *Smyth & Helwys Bible Commentary: Hebrews–James* (Macon, GA: Smyth & Helwys Publishing, 2004).
[3] Charles Ryrie; Quoted by David Jeremiah in *The Jeremiah Study Bible* (Franklin, TN: 2013), p. 1747, footnote Hebrews 2:17.
[4] David Jeremiah, *The Jeremiah Study Bible* (Franklin, TN: 2013), p. 1747, footnote Hebrews 2:17.

Is it logical to put the needs of the many before the needs of the one? Why?

Can you see any other way to be restored to God without Jesus' sacrificial act? Why?

Is it possible to explain Jesus' sacrifice to someone who knows nothing about Him? Why?

WEEPING OVER JERUSALEM

And when he drew near and saw the city, he wept over it.—Luke 19:41

Gene and Carol Kent have been forced to face the devastating consequences of their child's decisions. Early one morning, they received the phone call that changed their lives—their son had been arrested for murder. Recounting their family's experience in her book, *When I Lay My Isaac Down*, Carol Kent said, "Without warning our dreams for our only child came crashing down in a thousand broken pieces. Our whole world felt shattered" (p. 17).[1]

Read Luke 19:37-44. Jesus entered Jerusalem to celebrate His final Passover with His disciples. All four gospels recorded that Jesus was simultaneously praised by the people and criticized by the Pharisees, who demanded that Jesus "rebuke" His followers. But only Luke recorded that Jesus wept over the city because He knew her inhabitants would suffer greatly for refusing to accept Him as their King.

The people of Jerusalem, the "city of peace," longed for peace but completely failed to recognize Jesus as their promised "Prince of peace" (Is. 9:6). The religious leaders had already rejected Jesus as the Messiah (v. 39), and soon the crowds would demand His execution (Lk. 23:20-23). Jesus wept because the people were blinded to the truth that had been revealed to them many times by the prophets. And when they rejected the Prince of peace, Jesus revealed details of their imminent destruction, which occurred less than forty years later. In A.D. 66, the Jews revolted against Rome, and the Romans retaliated by attacking Jerusalem, surrounding the city, and starving the people. In A.D. 70, the Romans destroyed the Temple and most of the city walls, and killed six hundred thousand Jews.

---

[1] Carol Kent, *When I Lay My Isaac Down: Unshakable Faith in Unthinkable Circumstances* (Colorado Springs: NavPress, 2004, 2013), p. 17.

How have you felt as you watched others make poor choices that would have significant consequences?

What efforts did you make to change their decisions? Why were your efforts ultimately unsuccessful?

How can you share with others the depth of Jesus' love for them, and the magnitude of His sorrow if they choose to reject His love?

WEEPING OVER JERUSALEM

O Jerusalem, Jerusalem, the city that kills the prophets and stones those who are sent to it! How often would I have gathered your children together as a hen gathers her brood under her wings, and you were not willing!—Luke 13:34

While watching the hens and chicks in her yard one day while a hawk circled overhead, Peggy Joyce Ruth made a surprising discovery: "That mother hen did not run to those little chicks and jump on top of them to try to cover them with her wings. No! Instead, she squatted down, spread out her wings and began to cluck. And those little chickens, from every direction, came running to her to get under those outstretched wings. Then, the hen pulled her wings down tight, tucking every little chick safely under her."[1]

Read Luke 13:31-35. Like the prophets in previous generations, Jesus healed the sick and clearly communicated God's Word to His people. And, like the people in previous generations, the religious leaders refused to accept His message. In fact, previous generations had killed the prophets and stoned those God sent to them. This generation tried to chase Jesus out of town, claiming that Herod wanted to kill Him. But Jesus wasn't just a prophet—He was God's own Son who had come to earth to reveal the depth of God's love for all people. Regardless of the opposition, He would accomplish the redemptive work He had come to do.

Jesus then expressed His sadness for the many ways that the Jews had refused to respond to Him. Although Jesus longed to gather His people to Himself "as a hen gathers her chicks under her wings," once again, the Jews rejected Him.

Like the chicks in the barnyard that ran under the hen's wings for protection, we have the privilege of running to Jesus for salvation. If we refuse to seek shelter under His wings, we will be forever separated from Him.

---

[1] Peggy Joyce Ruth, *Psalm 91: Real-Life Stories of God's Shield of Protection* (Lake Mary, FL: Charisma House, 2010), p. 26.

Are there people in your life whom you long to gather close and protect? How do you feel when they reject you?

In what ways have you rejected Jesus' protection over your life? Based on this passage, can you envision how Jesus' mourns over your decision?

How would you describe the security you feel as one who is beloved and protected by Jesus?

WEEPING OVER JERUSALEM

But turning to them Jesus said, "Daughters of Jerusalem, do not weep for me, but weep for yourselves and for your children."—Luke 23:28

After Princess Diana was killed in a car wreck in 1997, thousands of people flocked to London to leave flowers outside the gates of Kensington Palace while openly weeping over her death. Although the mourners hadn't known Diana personally, for days they publicly expressed their sorrow over her tragic and untimely death.

Read Luke 23:26-31. These verses contain Jesus' third lament over Jerusalem. As He was led to the cross, Jesus was followed by a group of women who mourned and wailed for Him. Both MacArthur and Thomas explained these were not the women of Galilee who had closely followed Jesus during His ministry, but were professional mourners who wailed and wept whenever condemned Jews were led to their deaths.[1] *Gill's Exposition of the Entire Bible* offered several reasons why Jesus told the women not to cry for Him. First, Jesus was prepared to die because this was what He had come to do. Second, Jesus wasn't afraid to die because the pain would not last and death would not hold Him. Third, Jesus knew He would be raised again to sit at His Father's right hand in heaven. Fourth, Jesus knew that His sacrificial death would fulfill the Law and satisfy God's requirements for justice, providing the way for people to be restored to God. With all of this in mind, Jesus told the women to cry for themselves and their children because the nation of Israel would soon suffer God's judgment for their sins—particularly the sin of rejecting and crucifying Him.[2]

Even as He walked the streets of Jerusalem to the cross, Jesus wept over Israel because the Jews had rejected Him and demanded His death even though they had been given every opportunity to believe in Him. He wept because they would suffer greatly for these offenses. Today we have the option of accepting or rejecting Jesus. He still weeps for those who turn away from Him because He knows the consequences they will suffer.

---

[1] John MacArthur, "Characters on the Road to the Cross, Part 2," available from https://www.gty.org/library/sermons-library/42-284/characters-on-the-road-to-the-cross-part-2; and Geoff Thomas, "The Wailing Women of Jerusalem," available from http://www.alfredplacechurch.org.uk/index.php/sermons/luke1/chapter-23/2327-31-the-wailing-women-of-jerusalem/.

[2] John Gill, *Gill's Exposition of the Entire Bible*; available from http://biblehub.com/commentaries/gill/luke/23.htm.

What purpose does weeping and mourning serve in our lives? When is a public display of mourning appropriate or inappropriate?

These women wept over Jesus' death for the wrong reasons. When have you wept over your sins for the wrong reasons? What are the right reasons to weep over sin?

How can you explain to others that Jesus weeps for those who reject Him because He knows what they will suffer?

WEEPING OVER JERUSALEM

For the wound of the daughter of my people is my heart wounded; I mourn, and dismay has taken hold on me.—Jeremiah 8:21

In 2015, Pixar Animation Studios released the movie *Inside Out*, which explored five emotions battling inside Riley Andersen, a young girl adjusting to new surroundings after her family's move. While joy was her dominant emotion, Riley also experienced sadness, anger, fear, and disgust. Dr. Lisa Firestone explained that experiencing sadness that results from pain or loss has real benefits. "Sadness is a live emotion that can serve to remind us of what matters to us, what gives our life meaning."[1]

Read Jeremiah 8:18-22. Jeremiah has frequently been called the "weeping prophet" because his deep love for his nation of Judah caused him to weep for the suffering she would experience because of her rebellion against God. Judah now faced the invading Babylonian army, and her destruction was imminent (Jer. 8:1-17). Terence Fretheim asserted that "the lamenting prophet embodies the words of a lamenting God. . . . [so] that we hear a cacophony of mourning at Israel's destruction."[2] Jeremiah was grief-stricken and heartsick over what would happen to the people because they rejected God to worship carved images and foreign gods. He wept fountains of tears because his people would be slain (Jer. 9:1). His tears were a constant reminder of his love for a people who had failed to love God.

We've examined three instances when Jesus wept over the city of Jerusalem because the nation would once again suffer terrible destruction for rejecting God. Many biblical scholars connect Jesus' grief with the grief of the lamenting God described in Jeremiah 8:21. Although Jesus, the Great Physician, had come to restore the health of His people, they refused to accept the healing He offered.

---

[1] Lisa Firestone, "The Value of Sadness," available from https://www.psychologytoday.com/blog/compassion-matters/201507/the-value-sadness.
[2] Terence E. Fretheim, *Smyth & Helwys Bible Commentary: Jeremiah* (Macon, GA: Smyth & Helwys Publishing, 2002), p. 148.

What similarities do you see between our nation today and the nation of Israel in both Jeremiah's time and in Jesus' time? Do you think Jesus weeps over our nation? Why?

What emotions do you feel when you think about the ways that our nation has rejected God and the healing offered by His Son?

Pause to write your prayer for our nation and/or for the people you know who refuse to accept the love that Jesus so freely offers.

CLEANSING THE TEMPLE

He said to them, "It is written, 'My house shall be called a house of prayer,' but you make it a den of robbers."—Matthew 21:13

One of the worst nightmares parents face begins when their child is old enough to attend worship. Most parents worry if their child will behave, if they will be able to even hear the sermon, and how their child's actions might impact the other worshippers around them. Trying to keep the child quiet and entertained while participating in worship may not just seem like an impossibility, but sadly becomes a reality as parents spend their time focused on their children.

Read Matthew 21:12-17. Jesus went to the Temple and was overcome with anger at the abuses He saw there. Consider these inappropriate actions. First, although there were four markets where worshippers could buy the elements to use in sacrifices, the high priest had allowed a market to be set up in the Court of the Gentiles within the Temple complex. This market created so much commotion that Gentile worshippers were unable to worship. Second, money changers were also a part of the market and charged inflated fees for converting foreign currency into special temple coins to pay the Temple tax. And the sale of doves, which even the poorest of worshippers could afford, created chaos as sellers tried to keep the birds from escaping their cages during the transaction.[1] The Temple had become a place of business rather than worship. Jesus became angry not only at the merchants but also the religious leaders who had allowed the abuse to begin and to continue.

Jesus was rightly angry about the way the actions of those who abused the sanctity of the Temple had impacted worshippers. He was angry that chaos had been allowed to enter a place of worship. He was angry that greed dominated the decisions that were being made within the Temple. He was angry that the religious leaders, as well as the merchants and the money changers, were getting richer while taking advantage of God's people. He conveyed His anger by throwing out the merchants and the money changers and restoring the Temple to what it was meant to be.

---

[1]Grant R. Osborne and Philip W. Comfort, *Life Application Bible Commentary: Matthew*, Carol Stream: IL, Tyndale House Publishers, 1996, p. 412.

Have you seen behaviors in worship that took your attention away from God? Why did those behaviors seem inappropriate to you?

How can you keep your attention on God during worship, regardless of what is going on around you?

How is God dishonored when places of worship are abused and defiled?

CLEANSING THE TEMPLE

And every pot in Jerusalem and Judah shall be holy to the Lord of hosts, so that all who sacrifice may come and take of them and boil the meat of the sacrifice in them. And there shall no longer be a trader in the house of the Lord of hosts on that day.—Zechariah 14:21

When the great nineteenth-century preacher Charles H. Spurgeon reflected on today's passage from Zechariah, the message became incredibly personal for him. He wrote that since he had already experienced the day of the Lord in his life, everything in his life should be holy to God—what he wore each day would become a reminder of putting on the righteousness of Christ, and his meals would remind him of God's provision. He went on, "Oh, that today my clothes may be vestments, my meals sacraments, my house a temple, my table an altar, my speech incense, and myself a priest! Lord, fulfill thy promise, and let nothing be to me common or unclean."[1]

Read Zechariah 14:20-21. The last chapter of the book of Zechariah describes the coming day of the LORD or YHWH, often referred to as the second coming. Verses 20-21 picture the time when the Temple and the city of Jerusalem are both holy, sanctified places. The writer describes how even the horses of war would wear decorative bells that were engraved with the same words (Holy to the Lord) as the high priest wore on a plaque on his turban to indicate that they, too, were holy unto God.[2] Even the utensils used in cooking would be recognized as being holy and set apart for the worship of the LORD just as much as the utensils used as a part of sacrifices to God. One commentator wrote, "In short, everything within Jerusalem will be consecrated and become as holy as the temple, and the entire temple will become as sacred as the holy of holies."[3]

When Jesus confronted the abuse within the Temple, He might have thought of this passage and its promise that God would be honored throughout all of Jerusalem. If so, His anger could have grown from His discouragement over just how far the religious leaders and the people of Judah had moved away from what God had intended.

---

[1] Charles H. Spurgeon, *Zechariah-Spurgeon Devotionals & Sermon Notes*; available on-line at http://www.preceptaustin.org/zechariah_sermon_illustrations.
[2] *The Archaeological Study Bible*; Grand Rapids, MI: Zondervan Publishing, 2005, p. 1544, footnote 14:20.
[3] James D. Nogalski, *Smyth & Helwys Bible Commentary: The Book of the Twelve; Micah–Malachi*; Macon, GA: 2011, pp. 980-981.

What does it mean to be a holy people? A holy person?

Can you imagine a time when your church and your community became a holy place? If not, what might that look like?

Does thinking about the second coming of Christ impact the way you live today? Why?

CLEANSING THE TEMPLE

"These I will bring to my holy mountain, and make them joyful in my house of prayer; their burnt offerings and their sacrifices will be accepted on my altar; for my house shall be called a house of prayer for all peoples."—Isaiah 56:7

One of the most exclusive golf clubs in the United States is Augusta National located in Augusta, Georgia. The club hosts the Masters Golf Tournament each year during which Americans are treated to the beauty of the pristine golf course, the tall Georgia pines, and the blooming azaleas. What is less known about the club is what it takes to become a member. Although the club does not share the information, some reports suggest that the 300 members must be both wealthy and accomplished, and can pay between $25,000 and $50,000 a year in fees. The club is said to have a waiting list of 300 at any time, and new candidates must be nominated by a member.[1]

Read Isaiah 56:1-7. Isaiah began with the indictment that the people had not kept the law of the Sabbath and their lifestyle did not represent God (vv. 1-2). Isaiah also promised that God would bring all those who kept the Sabbath and accepted His covenant to be a part of His people (see vv. 3, 6). These people, the foreigners who had become proselytes, and the eunuchs who had been banned from participating in the worship of God (see Dt. 23:1-8), were promised inclusion rather than exclusion in God's presence on the mountain and in His "house of prayer," and granted fellowship with Him at His altar.[2] Their acceptance was based on their decision to follow Him (v. 7). This promise had eschatological (which can be understood as referring to the end times) impact as well, as it pointed to who would be included in God's coming Kingdom.[3]

Often the Old Testament is viewed through the lens of exclusivity of the Hebrew or the Jewish people. But when read in context, the Old Testament points to the inclusive nature of faith—all who call upon the name of Christ will be saved and become a part of God's Kingdom, will be accepted at God's altar, and will be given the opportunity to participate in the holy worship of God.

---

[1] Coleman McDowell, *Everything you need to know about becoming a member at August National*; available online at http://www.golf.com/tour-and-news/augusta-national-golf-club-membership.
[2] J. Alex Motyer, *The Prophecy of Isaiah: An Introduction & Commentary*; Downers Grove, IL: InterVarsity Press, 1993, p. 467.
[3] Frank E. Gaebelein, gen. ed., *The Expositor's Bible Commentary: Isaiah, Jeremiah, Lamentations, Ezekiel*, vol. 6; Grand Rapids, MI: Zondervan Publishing, 1986, p. 315

Who is excluded from worship today? Why?

What causes people to feel that they cannot take part in worshipping God? Are their feelings warranted? Why?

What do you think the Kingdom of God will look like when Jesus returns?

CLEANSING THE TEMPLE

"Has this house, which is called by my name, become a den of robbers in your eyes? Behold, I myself have seen it, declares the Lord."—Jeremiah 7:11

College football fans, especially those in the SEC, are rabid supporters of their teams. They'll pay huge amounts of money to procure tickets, participate in big tailgate parties even if they don't have tickets, and deck themselves out from head to toe in team gear. They'll scream until they lose their voices when their team is winning, and they're quick to turn those "cheers" into "boos" when the team doesn't step up to meet their expectations.

Read Jeremiah 7:1-11. The book of Jeremiah is really a record of God's conversation with His prophet. These verses are part of a larger passage (vv. 1-15) referred to as the Temple Sermon. God sent Jeremiah to His Temple with a message for those who came to worship there. Standing inside the gate to the Temple, Jeremiah proclaimed that the people needed to change their ways to continue to be allowed to dwell in God's House (v. 3). Read verse 4 carefully. Jeremiah delivered God's observation that the people participated in worship with a "mantra-like response," repeating the phrase over and over, and meaning none of it.[1] They, too, were quick to turn from worshipping God to just going through the motions. And God could tell the difference.

Jesus was a devoted student of God's Word, of the Torah, and the rest of the Old Testament. He showed His knowledge throughout His ministry, but no place in Scripture is it any more obvious than when Jesus cleared the Temple. Jesus recognized that those who should have been the most dedicated to God had allowed their focus and their decisions to move in directions that didn't include God's Word. Jesus was aware of their fickle nature and their quick changes of heart. And, when Jesus repeated these original words from God through His prophet Jeremiah in verse 11, He, too, added His admonition of the way God's House and His holy presence was being treated.

---

[1] Terence E. Fretheim, *Smyth & Helwys Bible Commentary: Jeremiah*. Macon, GA: Smyth & Helwys Publishing, 2002, pp. 131-133.

Are you able to pull teachings from the Old Testament to support your understanding of Jesus as God's Son? Is that important to you? Why?

In what ways do you allow your focus to move away from God during worship?

What message do you think God would want to deliver to your worshipping community?

CURSING THE FIG TREE

And seeing a fig tree by the wayside, he went to it and found nothing on it but only leaves. And he said to it, "May no fruit ever come from you again!" And the fig tree withered at once.—Matthew 21:19

Every gardener eventually faces the challenge of determining why trees won't bear fruit. Luckily, many print and Internet resources offer a list of things to evaluate: sunlight, temperature, air drainage, soil nutrients and drainage, best plant stock, controlling pests, disease and weeds, pruning, and fertilizing.[1] Unfortunately, when all efforts to improve growing conditions have been made, some plants still will not bear fruit. Then the gardener must decide if the unfruitful trees should be removed to make room for fruitful ones.

Read Matthew 21:18-22. After spending the night in Bethany, Jesus and His disciples returned to Jerusalem. When He saw a fig tree sporting leaves but no fruit, He capitalized on a teachable moment. When He cursed the fig tree, the disciples were stunned that it withered at once. Ben Witherington stressed that "the disciples continue[d] to be obtuse, showing no interest in the symbolic meaning of the withering of the fig tree but only being interested in how Jesus did it."[2] Through this visual parable, Jesus emphasized that the barren fig tree symbolized Israel's spiritual barrenness. By cursing the fruitless fig tree, Jesus revealed the coming judgment against Israel. As the disciples marveled at Jesus' actions, He emphasized that they could do this and more if they only prayed, having faith that God would respond.

Israel was the nation God had chosen to share Him with the world. Yet this chosen nation had been unfaithful to God and had failed to bear fruit for His Kingdom. By cursing this unfruitful fig tree, Jesus revealed that Israel would soon be judged for their unfaithfulness and unfruitfulness. But Jesus also promised the disciples that if they prayed faithfully and trusted God, they would become powerful and productive members of His Kingdom.

---

[1] North Carolina State Extension, "North Carolina Production Guide for Smaller Orchard Plantings," available from https://content.ces.ncsu.edu/north-carolina-production-guide-for-smaller-orchard-plantings.
[2] Ben Witherington, III, *Smyth & Helwys Bible Commentary: Matthew* (Macon, GA: Smyth & Helwys Publishing, 2006), p. 398.

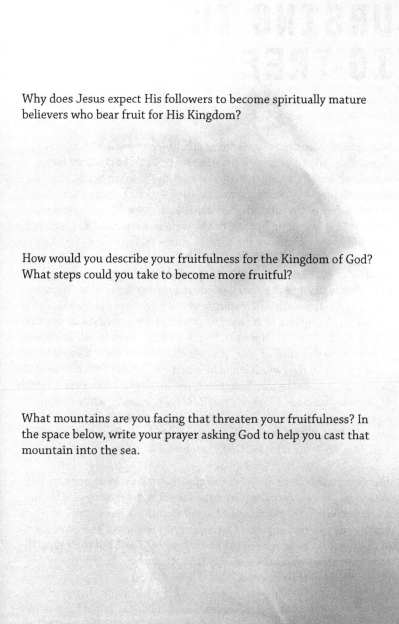

Why does Jesus expect His followers to become spiritually mature believers who bear fruit for His Kingdom?

How would you describe your fruitfulness for the Kingdom of God? What steps could you take to become more fruitful?

What mountains are you facing that threaten your fruitfulness? In the space below, write your prayer asking God to help you cast that mountain into the sea.

CURSING THE FIG TREE

Therefore I tell you, whatever you ask in prayer, believe that you have received it, and it will be yours.—Mark 11:24

Some people claim that skydiving is an unforgettable and exhilarating experience. After strapping a parachute onto their backs, they jump out of perfectly safe airplanes to plummet to the earth below, trusting the parachute will open on command to slow their fall and allow them to drift safely to the ground. Their faith in the parachute determines whether they will jump or cling to the seats in the plane. Without faith, they will never experience the thrill that free falling offers.

Read Mark 11:12-14, 20-25. Mark revealed that Jesus had cursed the tree one day and the disciples saw the results the next morning. Whether the tree withered instantly or overnight, we may wonder why Jesus cursed a fig tree that failed to produce fruit when "it was not the season for figs" (v. 13). However, fig trees in Israel produced two crops each year. By this time of year, the tree should have been covered with unripened early figs, which could be eaten even if they weren't sweet like fall season figs. In the Old Testament, productive fig trees were a symbol of peace in the land (1 Kgs. 4:25, Mic. 4:4, Zech. 3:10), while barren fig trees symbolized Israel's spiritual failures (Jer. 8:13, Mic. 7:1).[1] Yet, Israel had forsaken God and therefore could not produce fruit for His Kingdom, so Jesus revealed God's judgment.

Jesus also wanted His disciples to know that maintaining a strong faith in God was the essential requirement for doing great things for God's Kingdom. When the disciples dispersed from Jerusalem after Jesus' death and resurrection, their fervent prayers would be "the expression of unwavering confidence in the sovereignty of God" and their refusal to forgive others would be the only thing that would hinder the effectiveness of their prayers.[2]

After the destruction of the Temple, Jesus' followers would have to rely on prayer and their faith in God as they served Him. Walking with Jesus can be an exhilarating experience—if we have the faith to jump out of our comfort zones and boldly proclaim His name.

---

[1] R. Alan Culpepper, *Smyth & Helwys Bible Commentary: Mark* (Macon, GA: Smyth & Helwys Publishing, 2007), pp. 372-374.
[2] Ibid., pp. 381-383.

When is the proper season for a follower of Christ to bear fruit
for His Kingdom?

Why is faith in God the essential requirement for fruitful ministry?
How has God used your small faith to accomplish great things?

How can your faith be nourished so you can bear even more fruit for
God's Kingdom?

CURSING THE FIG TREE

"And he said to the vinedresser, 'Look, for three years now I have come seeking fruit on this fig tree, and I find none. Cut it down. Why should it use up the ground?'"—Luke 13:7

Whenever you hear the phrase "strike while the iron is hot," what comes to mind? The phrase originated in the fourteenth century, and was drawn from blacksmithing. Before the blacksmith could shape iron, he had to heat it in the fire until it glowed red-hot. While the iron was hot and malleable, the blacksmith had to work quickly to shape the iron. As the iron cooled, it hardened and once again become impossible to shape.[1] Obviously the phrase emphasizes the importance of responding to an opportunity quickly before it passes you by.

Read Luke 13:6-9. Luke also recorded an earlier occasion when Jesus used the common fig tree to illustrate spiritual truth. Within this parable of the fig tree, Jesus revealed several things. First, the nation Israel, like the fig tree, had been planted in a fertile and protected field. God had called His people out of slavery in Egypt and planted them in the Promised Land where He provided them with continual blessings. Despite those conditions, Israel was spiritually barren. They now had a very limited time to repent before Jesus would be crucified and they would face judgment. The remaining truths apply to individuals (rather than the nation as a whole). People who don't produce spiritual fruit will be judged, which could happen at any time because death often comes without warning. People should not delay responding to God because His patience will not last forever; God delays judgment because of His grace, not because people deserve more time to repent.[2]

The people of Israel had so often delayed their repentance and response to God that they had grown cold to His efforts to reach them. Even now, as Jesus walked among them, they rejected Him and demanded His death. God's patience with them had ended and they would soon suffer His judgment. Peter assured his readers that God is patient because He wants everyone to come to repentance (2 Pet. 3:9), but that, eventually, His judgment will come (2 Pet. 3:10). We would do well to respond quickly whenever we hear God's call.

---

[1] Betty Kirkpatrick, *Cliches: Over 1500 Phrases Explored and Explained* (New York: St. Martin's Press, 1996), p. 173.
[2] John MacArthur, *MacArthur New Testament Commentary: Luke 11-17* (Chicago: Moody Publishers, 2013), pp. 188-190.

Why does Jesus call people to quickly decide to place their faith in Him?

When have you delayed your response to Jesus' call? What opportunities have been lost because of your delay? What impact did that have on your obedient response to Him in later situations?

Who do you know that is delaying their repentance and response to God? Write out your prayers below for them.

CURSING THE
FIG TREE

When I would gather them, declares the Lord, there are no grapes on the vine, nor figs on the fig tree; even the leaves are withered, and what I gave them has passed away from them.—Jeremiah 8:13

In the world of competitive sports, from Pee Wee football to the NFL, from Little League to MLB, every team must obey the rules of their sports organization. The coaches have the responsibility of clearly explaining the rules of the game to all players on the team, and then ensuring all players follow those rules. If the coach decides the rules don't apply to his team and allows the players to continually break them, eventually the team will be disqualified from play and stripped of any titles they may have won.

Read Jeremiah 8:8-13. In these verses, Jeremiah, speaking for God, addressed the religious leaders (the scribes) of Israel, who were responsible for studying the Law and leading the people to obey. These scribes claimed to know the Law, yet they presented false information to the people. Feinberg said the scribes "manipulated the law of God as to falsify its message. They interpreted it in such a way as to assure the people that they could sin with impunity. . . . They twisted it to make it mean what they wanted it to."[1] God exposed both their abuse of His Word as well as their refusal to be ashamed for misleading the people. Because the prophets and priests practiced deceit, God promised to take away everything He had given them (v. 13).

Just like the scribes in Jeremiah's day, the religious leaders of Jesus' day were guilty of abusing the Law and misleading the people (see Mt. 23:1-4). Jesus followed in God's footsteps when He condemned Israel for failing to bear spiritual fruit. It should be noted, however, that when God brings judgment upon those who forsake Him, He does so with grief and sorrow. If we wish to avoid this judgment, then we must faithfully study God's Word and accurately share its truths with others.

---

[1]Charles L. Feinberg, "Jeremiah," in *The Expositor's Bible Commentary: Isaiah, Jeremiah, Lamentations, Ezekiel*, vol. 6 (Grand Rapids, MI: Zonderan Publishing), p. 436.

Why is God angered when people intentionally twist His Word to mean what they want it to mean?

What responsibilities do parents have for teaching spiritual truths to their children? What responsibilities do ministers have for teaching spiritual truths to their congregation?

How can the proper interpretation of God's Word bring health and healing to people? What steps can you take to do this?

FACING HIS OPPOSITION

And Jesus said to them, "Neither will I tell you by what authority I do these things."—Luke 20:8

Authority is given. For example, the President of the United States is given authority to lead the country that is governed by the Constitution of the United States. Or, the CEO of a major corporation is given authority to lead the work of the company that is governed by the Board of Directors. Their authority is given, overseen, and temporary. Their authority can, at any time, be taken away.

Read Luke 20:1-8. Jesus' difficulties with the religious leaders increased during His last week in Jerusalem. After Jesus cleared the Temple, a group of religious leaders came to Jesus and asked Him upon what authority He had acted. Basically, their question was, What gives you the right to do this? What they meant was, Where does your authority come from? They implied that Jesus had not received permission or authority from them, so He was guilty of treason—a crime against Rome. If Jesus didn't respond with words of treason, they hoped He would respond with statements of blasphemy.[1] Instead, Jesus asked them a question: Where did John the Baptist's authority to baptize come from? Once again, Jesus silenced His critics. They could not answer without causing more problems for themselves. When they responded that they didn't know where John's authority came from, Jesus answered, "Neither will I tell you by what authority I do these things" (v. 8).

Jesus forced the religious leaders into a corner over whether John had received his authority from God or had taken it upon himself. The leaders realized that if they acknowledged John's authority from God, they became foolish because they refused to listen to him. However, if they said that John had taken on the authority on his own initiative, the crowds who had seen God's work in John would rebel against them. They took the easy way out. This debate continues today. Is Jesus the Son of God who has all the authority of God to act? Or, is Jesus a good man who showed us how to live? Our answer to those questions will determine our eternity in heaven.

---

[1]Grant Osborne and Philip W. Comfort, eds. *Life Application Bible Commentary: Luke.* Carol Stream, IL: Tyndale House Publishers, 1997, pp. 447-448.

Can you understand what the religious leaders were attempting to do?

Who do you say Jesus is? From whom does He receive His authority?

How would you respond to those who questioned Jesus' authority?
Would you have been interested or infuriated? Why?

FACING HIS OPPOSITION

So Jesus said to them, "When you have lifted up the Son of Man, then you will know that I am he, and that I do nothing on my own authority, but speak just as the Father taught me."—John 8:28

Recently, scammers have found ways to present themselves as known merchants on Facebook. Facebook users receive a link to a company's "website" that actually belongs to the scammers, who use it to grab personal information from the Facebook user's order. Facebook users have felt secure in ordering from companies they know and trust, only to find out they've been tricked into believing a lie. Their sense of security has been damaged by these Facebook scammers who have abused their trust in a recognized company.

Read John 8:21-30. The religious leaders tried to set Jesus up by bringing a woman caught in adultery before Him (Jn. 7:53–8:11). They asked Jesus to decide if the woman was guilty or not, again pushing Him to proclaim Himself in such a way that they could bring charges against Him. Instead, Jesus pushed each of the accusers to look at the sin in their own lives first. The accusers left without carrying out the sentence of stoning on the woman, and Jesus continued to teach in the Temple. The religious leaders pushed Jesus again, asking who gave Him authority to act in an attempt to show that Jesus was the trickster, the one who presented a lie that was beginning to convince others that He was authentic. Beginning in John 8:21, Jesus explained that He was the real thing because He had been sent by God, His Father. Jesus emphasized that, because God is reliable, His Son was also reliable. Further, Jesus stressed that He did nothing—in actions or in words—that did not come directly from God.

We've become aware of scammers . . . people who want to trick us. If they're successful, they can steal our identities, our money, and our sense of security. It can be easy to allow that growing sense of unease from trying to navigate our world to impact our faith as well. Yet, Jesus is not a myth or a scam, He's not an invention of the early Christian community, and He's not just a good person whom we can emulate in our lives. Jesus is the one and only, unique and much loved, Son of God who came to the world to take on our sins so we could be restored back to His Father.

Have you ever thought that accepting Jesus as Savior and Lord was a scam? Why or why not?

What would it mean to you if Jesus was only a good person whose life showed us how to live?

How would you respond to those who claim that belief in Jesus as the Christ is a scam?

FACING HIS OPPOSITION

"No one takes it from me, but I lay it down of my own accord. I have authority to lay it down, and I have authority to take it up again. This charge I have received from my Father."—John 10:18

The United States Marine Corps trains under the motto, "No man left behind," and there are plenty of stories of how individual Marines upheld that task. One story is about Sgt. Kenneth A. Altazan, a Vietnam veteran. On a medical evacuation mission, Altazan left the helicopter to help wounded Marines make it to the copter. Although Altazan was hit in the knee, he still managed to get two men back to safety. In his final extraction, in pain from his wound, he threw off his body armor so he could get two more Marines back to safety. He received the Navy Cross in 2015 for his actions. His Navy Cross citation states that "his bold initiative and selfless concern helped save the lives of his fellow Marines, inspired all who observed him and was instrumental in completing the hazardous mission."[1]

Read John 10:17-18. At the beginning of chapter 10, Jesus began to deliver what some call His "discourse on the Good Shepherd,"[2] in which Jesus stressed the care and concern of the Shepherd for His sheep. In verse 14, Jesus identified Himself as the good Shepherd, and then in verses 17-18, Jesus explained what He had come to do—to lay down His life and then pick it up again. *The Expositor's Bible Commentary* emphasizes that these verses relay two important pieces of information. First, Jesus' sacrificial act on the cross would be totally voluntary, and therefore, was nothing that any human could cause to happen. Second, Jesus had the authority to lay down His life at His will, and then pick it up again. In this picture of both His death and His resurrection, Jesus emphasized that He would do what no one else could do. "Anyone can lay down his life, if that means simply the termination of physical existence; but only the Son of the Father could at will resume his existence."[3]

Marines are committed to bringing back their comrades' bodies, whether dead or alive. In their efforts, many lose their own lives. But these courageous Marines do not have the ability to bring themselves or someone else back to life. Only Jesus has the power over life and death. Only Jesus could determine the time of His own death, as well as His resurrection. Only Jesus voluntarily gave His life for us.

---

[1] Cpl. Gabrielle Quire, "No Man Left Behind"; available on-line at http://www.marforres.marines.mil/Marine-Reserve-News-Photos/Marine-Reserve-News/Article/624452/no-marine-left-behind/.
[2] Frank E. Gaebelein, *The Expositor's Bible Commentary: John and Acts,* vol. 9 (Grand Rapids, MI: Zondervan Publishing, 1981), p. 107.
[3] Ibid., p. 110.

How does Jesus' statement that He has the power to give up His life and to bring it back confirm that He is the Son of God?

Jesus voluntarily accepted the pain and torture involved in being crucified. How does that demonstrate the depth of His love for all mankind?

How would you explain Jesus' power to someone who does not know Him?

FACING HIS OPPOSITION

"Jesus answered him, "You would have no authority over me at all unless it had been given you from above. Therefore he who delivered me over to you has the greater sin."—John 19:11

Dr. Thomas Chalmers was a career mathematician in the late 1700s. In his work, he encountered what he saw as the two great magnitudes in life—the brevity of life and the enormity of eternity. He was unable to explain those two opposing magnitudes in any way other than through the presence of the creator God. His revelation led him to become a minister and preacher in the Church of Scotland.

Read John 19:1-11. Jesus appeared before Pilate in what appeared to be a weak position. He had been bound and beaten. He was brought before Pilate, the man with the highest authority in Israel, as a prisoner by those who depended upon Pilate to condemn Him as a trouble maker and a blasphemer. The situation was based on whose authority was the greatest. The Jewish religious leaders counted on Pilate to see Jesus the way they did, and knew he had the authority to condemn Jesus to death. But Pilate didn't see things as they did. Pilate recognized that Jesus was innocent. He tried to appease the crowds and the Jewish leadership by having Jesus flogged. Instead, the crowds called for Jesus' crucifixion, demanding that Pilate take the final step in having Jesus killed. In verse 12, the crowds questioned whether Pilate was really committed to his position under Caesar if he refused to condemn Jesus. Pilate even looked for a way to release Jesus, and questioned Him about who He was. Jesus refused to answer. Eventually, Pilate gave in to the demands of the crowd, and according to Matthew, would take no credit for sentencing Jesus to death (Mt. 27:24).

Throughout his entire encounter with Jesus, Pilate agonized over the magnitude of the decision he had to make. He mistakenly thought that he had the authority of life and death over Jesus. The reality was that no person had any authority over Jesus. Jesus saw Pilate as "checked by the hand of God," having no power over Him beyond being "an instrument in the divine purpose" that unfolded before him.

---

[1] David Arnold, "60 Seconds–Eternity"; available on-line at http://globalchristiancenter.com/1126-english/devotionals/daily-devotions/60-seconds/33777-60-seconds-eternity.
[2] Frank E. Gaebelein, *The Expositor's Bible Commentary: John and Acts*, vol. 9 (Grand Rapids, MI: Zondervan Publishing, 1981), p. 176.

Reflect on Chalmers' two magnitudes. Do these point you to God as the Creator and Sustainer of all life? Why?

When you consider the authority that Jesus has over your life, how does that make you feel?

If you had been part of the crowd that watched Jesus' trial, how would you have responded?

FACING HIS OPPOSITION

And Jesus came and said to them, "All authority in heaven and on earth has been given to me."—Matthew 28:18

People with authority can inspire us or intimidate us. They can build us up or tear us down. They can motivate us to become the people we are meant to be, or they can reduce us into a mere shadow of what God intended. Someone with authority can be a gift, a reward, and a blessing in our lives. Or, someone in authority, who is consumed with power and personal agendas, can stop at nothing to get what he or she wants. If we are caught in the fall-out, we can be hurt emotionally, damaged psychologically, and left questioning everything about ourselves. In Jesus' time of temptation in the wilderness at the beginning of His ministry, Satan attempted to attack Jesus' authority, His purpose on earth, and His commitment to see that purpose fulfilled.

Read Matthew 28:16-20. After His resurrection, Jesus returned to His disciples with a reminder of His authority. Jesus stated that He has "all authority in heaven and on earth." That means that His authority is lacking nothing. His authority is complete over the entire world. His authority is absolute, to which nothing can be added. And, it is that complete, total authority that He placed His followers under, instructing them to work in His authority. Compare that with Satan's temptation of Jesus in the wilderness. Satan showed Jesus the kingdoms of the world and then said, "All these I will give you" (Mt. 4:8). Interesting, isn't it, that Satan tempted Jesus with something he didn't have and Jesus didn't need? Jesus already had all authority; Satan had none.

Jesus' authority comes from God, because He, too, is God. His authority gives Him power over all things and brings glory to God. Within His authority, we can be who God intended us to be. Under His authority, we have the power to accomplish God's purpose here on earth. And, because of His authority, we will spend eternity with Him.

How have you experienced authority in a positive way and in a negative way?

Review the description of things we can experience through someone in authority. Do these resonate with you? Why?

How do you see Jesus' authority as the Son of God influencing your life?

SHARING THE SIGNS OF THE END TIMES

As he sat on the Mount of Olives, the disciples came to him privately, saying, "Tell us, when will these things be, and what will be the sign of your coming and of the end of the age?"—Matthew 24:3

Signs provide such an important function in our lives that we rely on them in many different types of situations. During many types of ballgames, players and coaches use hand signs to communicate with each other. When we travel to work or on vacation, we rely on road signs to guide us to our destination and warn us of any dangers along the way. Investors rely on economic signs to know when to invest in a business or stock fund and when to reclaim their funds. Our bodies provide physical signs that warn us of dangerous medical conditions that could threaten our lives. Even animals, both domesticated and wild, signal their intent to attack by posturing and growling.

Read Matthew 24:1-14. As Jesus and the disciples left the Temple for the last time, Jesus predicted that the Temple buildings would soon be destroyed so completely that "there will not be left here one stone upon another" (v. 2). Alone with Jesus later, the disciples asked Him for "the sign" that would precede this destruction, Jesus' coming, and the end of the age. In response, Jesus described several things that would happen: (1) others would claim to be Christ and lead many astray; (2) wars and rumors of wars would pit nation against nation; (3) famines and earthquakes would occur; (4) believers would be hated and put to death; (5) many believers would "fall away" and betray those who remained faithful; (6) sin and lawlessness would increase; and (7) the gospel would be preached throughout the whole world.

When today's followers of Christ compare these signs with events occurring in the world today, many wonder if "the end of the age" might be fast approaching. Because we know that Jesus predicted these things, we can take His words to heart, "See that you are not alarmed, for this must take place" (v. 6). We don't have to fear these signs, but should allow them to remind us to trust fully in Him.

Of the signs that Jesus described, which have you seen or heard of?

Do you find it comforting that Jesus' predicted these things would happen before the end? Why or why not?

How should the knowledge that Jesus is coming again impact the way you live each day?

SHARING THE SIGNS OF THE END TIMES

Therefore you also must be ready, for the Son of Man is coming at an hour you do not expect.—Matthew 24:44

Security companies exist to protect businesses and homes from thieves that break in without warning and steal company assets or valuable personal possessions. These companies promise their customers protection and peace of mind if they will just install door and window alarms, security cameras, and comprehensive control systems that are monitored twenty-four hours a day. And customers buy the systems to protect their assets because thieves don't announce when they will invade any business or home.

Read Matthew 24:29-31, 36-44. Just as we speak of earth-shaking news or catastrophic events, Jesus described the earth-shaking events that will occur when He returns. His comment that "the powers of the heavens will be shaken" (v. 29) could refer to literal cosmic events or to His overthrow of demonic spiritual forces.[1] When this happens, the Son of Man will appear and all the tribes of the earth will mourn, for Jesus will come to rescue His followers while judging and condemning others. Jesus then emphasized that no one—no humans, no angels, not even Jesus—knows when He will return. Only God, the One who "made the divine plan," knows exactly when Jesus will return, so believers must be ready at all times.[2] Until that day, people will continue to experience both the mundane daily and the joyful landmark events of life while waiting for Jesus to return. He will come unannounced and the unbelievers will be "taken" or "swept away" in judgment.[3] By calling believers to remain alert and ready, Jesus stressed the importance of remaining faithful to Him.

Rather than trying to predict the exact moment of Jesus' return, believers are called to be faithful followers of Christ who continually live in connection with Him. In this way, regardless of when Jesus returns, we will be ready and waiting for Him.

---

[1] Craig L. Blomberg, *The New American Commentary: Matthew* (Nashville: Broadman Press, 1992), p. 362.
[2] Ben Witherington, *Smyth & Helwys: Matthew* (Macon, GA: Smyth & Helwys Publishers, 2006), p. 454.
[3] Blomberg, p. 366, and Witherington, p. 455.

What did Jesus say would happen when He returns? At what time will this occur?

What indication did Jesus give that people—even believers—would be surprised by His return? Why did He challenge His followers to remain alert and ready?

Since Jesus has delayed His return for so long, has the Church become complacent? What can individual believers do to remain alert and ready?

SHARING THE SIGNS OF THE END TIMES

I saw in the night visions, and behold, with the clouds of heaven there came one like a son of man, and he came to the Ancient of Days and was presented before him.—Daniel 7:13

Take a few moments to list the three to five things about your future that you worry about the most. How do you think your list compares with the items on other people's lists? Why do people from different stages of life worry about the same things? For example, young adults might worry about having enough money to pay the bills while older adults worry about having enough money to survive retirement. What other common concerns about the future do you think people of all ages, ethnicities, and economic conditions share?

Read Daniel 7:9-13. Jesus continued teaching throughout His last week in Jerusalem. In Matthew 24, He answered the disciples' questions about how to recognize the signs of the end of the age. When Jesus referred to Himself as the Son of Man, perhaps they remembered Daniel's prophecies about the Son of Man. During the latter years of his life, Daniel had a dream of four great beasts who were defeated by the Ancient of Days (vv. 11-12). Then, "one like a son of man" was presented before the Ancient of Days, who gave Him "dominion and glory and a kingdom" so that people from every nation would serve Him (v. 14a). This kingdom would last forever. Unlike the transient and ever-changing kingdoms of this world, the Son of Man's kingdom would never be destroyed or pass away (v. 14b). Daniel clearly described the time when God would grant full authority over all the world to His beloved Son. Compare Daniel's prophecy with Jesus' explanation of His return in Matthew 24:30.

Have you ever heard the phrase, "I don't know what the future holds, but I know who holds the future"? Even though we don't know what might happen next year, next week, or even tomorrow, we can rest assured that we know the One who holds the future. When we trust in Jesus, we know that our ultimate future is secure even if we must face disappointment, hardship, persecution, and death in this world.

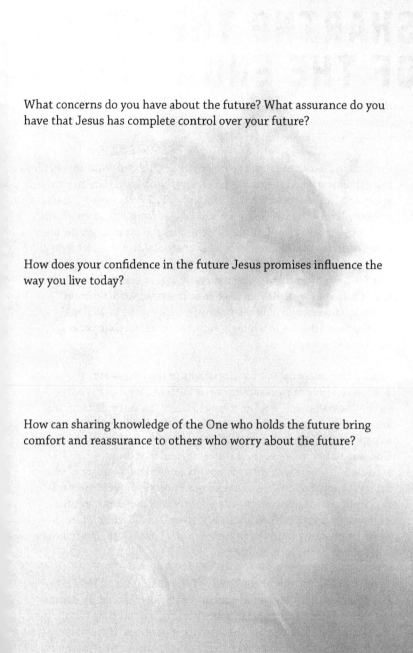

What concerns do you have about the future? What assurance do you have that Jesus has complete control over your future?

How does your confidence in the future Jesus promises influence the way you live today?

How can sharing knowledge of the One who holds the future bring comfort and reassurance to others who worry about the future?

SHARING THE SIGNS OF THE END TIMES

To this end we always pray for you, that our God may make you worthy of his calling and may fulfill every resolve for good and every work of faith by his power.—2 Thessalonians 1:11

Professional athletes know the risk of injury, yet they continue to play the game; and when they are injured, they work hard to return to their sport as quickly as possible. On January 4, 2017, Montreal Canadiens hockey player Brendan Gallagher's hand was fractured when he was struck by a hockey puck. Ironically, this was the same finger on the same hand that was injured just a year before. After the first injury, Gallagher underwent surgery and rehab before returning to play in just 40 days. After this second injury, Gallagher endured surgery to insert a second steel plate in his hand. This time, he determined to work hard enough in rehab to return to his sport in 39 days.[1] What drives athletes to willingly suffer such injuries, surgeries, and rehab regimens?

Read 2 Thessalonians 1:4-12. Christians in the first century suffered terrible persecution for their faith in Jesus. In his letter to the Thessalonians, Paul encouraged them to remain faithful and steadfast in the midst of such persecution so they would be found worthy of God's calling and glorify their Savior. Paul promised that God was not unaware of their suffering, and that Jesus, when He returned "from heaven with his mighty angels in flaming fire," would inflict "vengeance on those who do not know God" (vv. 7-8). Paul's description of Jesus was echoed in John's vision of Jesus' return in Revelation 19:11-16. While Jesus' enemies will suffer "eternal destruction, away from the presence of the Lord" (v. 9), His followers will forever be in His presence.

Jesus suffered terribly at the hands of His enemies, and He warned His disciples that they would also suffer terribly (Mt. 24:9). Because we have a Savior who understands suffering, we can cling faithfully to Him, trusting Him to judge those who persecute us. By remaining true to our faith even when facing persecution, we prove worthy of our calling and glorify our Lord.

---

[1] Joanie Godin, "Suffering for a cause," 14 January 2017, available from https://www.nhl.com/canadiens/news/brendan-gallagher-is-recovering-from-his-injury/c-285677604.

Why does the world persecute those who place their faith in Christ? What will ultimately happen to those who attack Christ's followers?

Why is it comforting to know that Jesus remained faithful to His mission despite the suffering He endured?

In what ways have you suffered because of your faith in Christ? What enables you to remain faithful during those times?

SHARING THE SIGNS OF THE END TIMES

Then I saw heaven opened, and behold, a white horse! The one sitting on it is called Faithful and True, and in righteousness he judges and makes war.
—Revelation 19:11

During the time of the Roman Empire, white horses were highly valued, and were therefore reserved for rulers, important officials, and triumphant military leaders returning to Rome.[1] After Julius Caesar returned from his victorious campaign in northern Africa, the Roman Senate permitted him to "drive a chariot drawn by four white horses" in his triumphal victory parade through Rome.[2]

Read Revelation 19:11-16. In this vision, John saw heaven open to reveal a rider on a white horse accompanied by the armies of heaven who also rode white horses. The appearance of this rider heralded victory for His followers and certain defeat for His enemies. The rider had eyes like fire, which meant that nothing could be hidden from Him. The many crowns on His head symbolized His majesty, strength, and authority. He wore a robe dipped in blood, the blood He shed on the cross to overcome and defeat His foes.[3] The imagery clearly portrays the rider as Jesus, whom John further identified as "Faithful and True," "The Word of God," and "King of kings and Lord of lords." This powerful rider employed a sharp sword to strike His enemies and a rod of iron to rule over them. Wilson stated, "Word as a title coupled with the imagery of the sword out of his mouth emphasizes the authority by which he declares that the nations are destroyed."[4]

Jesus came to earth the first time as a Suffering Servant who offered His life as the sacrifice for humanity's sins. But when Jesus returns at the end of the age, He will return as the conquering King over all creation who makes war against His enemies and judges the world in righteousness. As followers of Christ, we give thanks for His sacrifice and await His return with joyous anticipation.

---

[1] Craig S. Keener, *The NIV Application Commentary: Revelation* (Grand Rapids, MI: Zondervan Publishing House, 2000), p. 453.
[2] Mark Wilson, "Revelation," in *Zondervan Illustrated Bible Backgrounds Commentary: Hebrews to Revelation*, vol. 4 (Grand Rapids, MI: Zondervan Publishing House, 2002), p. 356.
[3] Leon Morris, *Tyndale New Testament Commentary*, 2nd ed. (Grand Rapids, MI: Wm. B. Eerdmans Publishing Company, 2000), pp. 223-4; and Wilson, p. 356.
[4] Wilson, p. 356.

How does Scripture contrast Jesus' return to earth at the end of the age with His first appearance? What is different about His mission this time?

What do the names of Jesus in this passage tell you about His identity and character?

How might your relationship with Jesus be impacted by your understanding of the events of "the end of the age"?

JESUS HAS RISEN

But the angel said to the women, "Do not be afraid, for I know that you seek Jesus who was crucified. He is not here, for he has risen, as he said."
—Matthew 28:5-6a

What parents have not had that moment when their child has disappeared from view in a busy store? Frustration quickly turns into panic as they desperately search for the child under clothing racks and behind columns. And, complete relief and joy takes over when they find the child safe. It only takes a moment before fear takes over when a precious child is lost or out of sight. Sadly, some children disappear and cannot be found, and the grief those parents experience can be inconsolable.

Read Matthew 28:1-10. Matthew recorded that Mary Magdalene and the other Mary, the mother of James and Joseph, went to the tomb early in the morning. He even stated that they were worried about how they would get into the tomb because they had watched Joseph of Arimathea seal the tomb with a large rock just before the Sabbath began (see Mt. 27:59-61). Why did Matthew include these details? Possibly because he wanted to show the irony that the women came expecting to find a dead body, not a risen Lord. Regardless of what they had been told, they still couldn't comprehend Jesus' resurrection. Also note that neither Matthew or Mark gave any details about Jesus' resurrection itself, but chose to include only the impact His resurrection had on His followers. The women were greeted by an angel who moved the stone and invited them to see where Jesus had been. As the women left the empty tomb, they encountered their risen Lord.

Instead of a sealed tomb, the women found an angel. Instead of a dead body, the women found an empty tomb. Instead of strong and courageous guards, the women saw men who were pale and trembling from fear. Instead of being panicked over their missing Lord, the women heard the news, "He is not here, for He has risen, just as He said." And instead of leaving in grief and desolation, the women left in joy and celebration because they had seen their risen Lord.

How would you have felt if you had approached the tomb with the women?

Why do you think it was difficult for the women to accept that death would not keep Jesus?

How do you experience joy at Easter?

JESUS HAS RISEN

Remember how he told you, while he was still in Galilee, that the Son of Man must be delivered into the hands of sinful men and be crucified and on the third day rise.—Luke 24:6b–7

A trip through the Gettysburg Battlefield Museum is eye opening. The museum has gathered eyewitness accounts, letters home, and battlefield reports from officers and soldiers on both sides of the Civil War. What is surprising is how differently people on both sides of the war reacted to their experiences. They saw the same battles from different perspectives, and those different perspectives led them to interpret what they had experienced differently. Historians regularly face this struggle of trying to accurately tell a story, document history, and interpret its meaning in order to teach people about that event or period in history.

Read Luke 24:1-8. Luke's account of the women going to the tomb provided some additional details that were not included in Matthew's account. First, Luke stated that the group of women included Mary Magdalene, Joanna, Mary the mother of James, and several other women, who had come with spices to prepare Jesus' body. Second, Luke shared that the stone had already been rolled away from the tomb entrance before the women arrived. Third, Luke stated the women entered the tomb to find it empty, and that when they left the tomb they found two angels there. Fourth, the angels reminded the women of Jesus' words, while still in Galilee, promising that He would rise from the dead. Fifth, the women went back to find the disciples to tell them what happened, but the disciples didn't believe them.

Luke and Matthew approached what happened at the empty tomb from different perspectives. Neither were there and had to depend on the witness of others to know what happened. Both chose which details to use and which to leave out in order to tell the most important event that would ever be recorded. Luke wanted to stress the surprise the women and the disciples experienced when they realized that Jesus wasn't dead. He was alive. And they hadn't believed that it was even possible!

Imagine being with the women and/or the disciples and finding out that Jesus wasn't dead. How would you have reacted to the news?

What would experiencing Jesus' resurrection first-hand have taught you about your faith?

Have you ever shared those feelings about your faith in Jesus the risen Lord with anyone? Why?

JESUS HAS RISEN

And if Christ has not been raised, then our preaching is in vain and your faith is in vain.—1 Corinthians 15:14

Antique Roadshow is a PBS series watched by more than 8.5 million people each week. On the show, people bring their treasures to have them appraised. Each person hopes that the item he or she brought will be worth millions. Sadly, few owners hear that what they have is so valuable. Why? In most cases, the authenticity of the item is questioned. Is the item real? Is it original? Has it been well preserved? All these elements impact the value of the item.

Read 1 Corinthians 15:12-19. Paul received word from the church in Corinth that some people were arguing that the story of Jesus' resurrection from the dead was not real. They didn't believe that Jesus was authentically raised from the dead. If that argument was accepted, it then negated the truth of Jesus' resurrection. So, Paul began to build his case, as carefully as any attorney, to prove that Jesus died on the cross and was raised from the dead. First, Paul listed all those who had seen Jesus alive after His death—Peter and then the disciples, more than 500 followers, James and then all the apostles, and then Paul himself (vv. 5-8). Hundreds had seen Jesus, had talked to Jesus and heard Him speak, and had witnessed His resurrection. Therefore, Paul asked, how could anyone deny His resurrection (v. 12)? Paul stressed that denying Jesus' resurrection meant that all preaching about Jesus was useless, the work of the disciples was worthless, and those who followed Jesus were to be pitied because their faith was false (v. 19).

The word "pitied" seems severe. Paul wanted his readers to understand that they were part of more than an earthly movement. Osborne and Comfort explains that there were few tangible benefits to following Christ in the first century. Instead, believers faced persecution from nonbelievers, banishment from their families, and even poverty. And, the believers would still be living in sin if Christ's resurrection had not happened.[1]

---

[1] Grant R. Osborne and Philip W. Comfort, *Life Application Bible Commentary: 1 & 2 Corinthians* (Carol Stream, IL: Tyndale Publishers, 1999), p. 226.

Would your faith be worthless without Jesus' resurrection as the cornerstone? Why?

How would you respond to someone who denied Jesus was resurrected from dead?

Do you feel pity for those who cannot accept the truth of Jesus' resurrection? Why?

JESUS HAS RISEN

But in fact Christ has been raised from the dead, the firstfruits of those who have fallen asleep.—1 Corinthians 15:20

Children "love" to play the "If" game, with questions like: *If Mommy got really mad at me, what would she do? If Mommy and Daddy get a divorce, would they stop loving me? What will happen if Daddy loses his job?* Usually, those questions communicate the fears the children are carrying, often based on what they've seen happen in friends' families.

Read 1 Corinthians 15:20-28. Paul responded to the "If" questions about Jesus' resurrection: *How can there be a true resurrection from the dead? What if Jesus wasn't ever really dead? What if Jesus didn't rise from the dead and it was all a myth?* To these questions, Paul answered resoundingly that the historical fact is that Jesus was raised from the dead. Osborne and Comfort recorded eight factual events that give evidence to Jesus' resurrection: (1) a Roman soldier announced Jesus' death (Mk. 15:44-45); (2) soldiers didn't break Jesus' legs because He was already dead (Jn. 19:32-34); (3) Joseph of Arimathea and Nicodemus handled Jesus' dead body (Jn. 19:38-42); (4) Mary Magdalene and the other Mary watched as Jesus' body was put into the tomb (Mt. 27:59-61, Mk. 15:47, Lk. 23:55); (5) Roman soldiers sealed the tomb; (6) Roman soldiers also guarded the tomb (Mt. 27:65-66); (7) two days later, the women went into the tomb and found it empty (Mt. 28:1-6); and (8) Peter and John went into the empty tomb (Jn. 20:3-9).[1]

Paul didn't stop with the fact of the resurrection, but continued with the identity of who Jesus is. Jesus is the *firstfruits*, the best of the harvest and a perfect gift from God. The image reminds Paul's readers that Jesus is the Lord of the harvest, and all believers can be confident of their own resurrection into eternity.[2] Belief in Jesus' resurrection provides comfort when a fellow believer passes away, and it creates grief when someone who is not a believer dies.

---

[1] Grant R. Osborne and Philip W. Comfort, *Life Application Bible Commentary: 1 & 2 Corinthians* (Carol Stream, IL: Tyndale Publishers, 1999), p. 227.
[2] Robash, *Smyth & Helwys Bible Commentary: 1 Corinthians* (Macon, GA: Smyth & Helwys Publishers, 2009, p. 404.

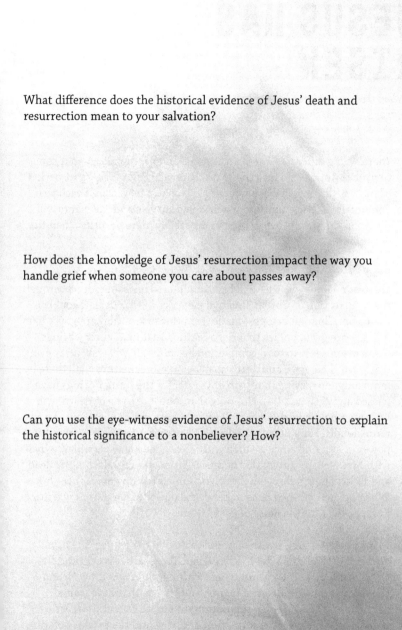

What difference does the historical evidence of Jesus' death and resurrection mean to your salvation?

How does the knowledge of Jesus' resurrection impact the way you handle grief when someone you care about passes away?

Can you use the eye-witness evidence of Jesus' resurrection to explain the historical significance to a nonbeliever? How?

JESUS HAS RISEN

When the perishable puts on the imperishable and the mortal puts on immortality, then shall come to pass the saying that is written: "Death is swallowed up in victory."—1 Corinthians 15:54

There's a big difference between annuals and perennials when it comes to plants. Annuals go into the ground and add color for a short period of time. Sadly, they'll die away, and will have to be replaced each year. Perennials die back, but the root systems survive and the plants will return in the spring, even larger and possibly more beautiful than the year before.

Read 1 Corinthians 15:50-57. Paul reminded his readers that their greatest enemy—death—had been conquered once and for all through the resurrection of Christ. The final evidence of that defeat would be seen when "human beings—made from the dust of the earth, just like Adam—are given bodies that defy death."[1] That final victory brings God's promises into total completion because "He will wipe away every tear from their eyes, and death shall be no more, neither shall there be mourning, nor crying, nor pain anymore, for the former things have passed away" (Rev. 21:4). Not only that, but "the sting of death" will no longer have control over believers. In Romans, Paul explained it in more detail: "For when we died with Christ we were set free from the power of sin. And since we died with Christ, we know we will also live with him. We are sure of this because Christ was raised from the dead, and He will never die again. Death no longer has any power over him. When he died, he died once to break the power of sin. But now that he lives, he lives for the glory of God." (Rom. 6:7-10)

Many people struggle with depression during the winter. The days are shorter, and darkness comes earlier. The weather is cold and the sky is often gray. Then, winter ends with new life, new growth, and the reappearance of flowers, plants, and shrubs that have waited throughout the winter for their dormant period to end. The earth itself is celebrating the resurrection of Christ and the promise of our own victory over death. And for those who have suffered from the winter blues, the promise of Jesus' resurrection is renewed.

---

[1] Grant R. Osborne and Philip W. Comfort, *Life Application Bible Commentary: 1 & 2 Corinthians* (Carol Stream, IL: Tyndale Publishers, 1999), p. 229.

Does the appearance of spring plants remind you of Christ's resurrection? Why?

How do you remember Jesus' resurrection each Easter?

How do you see Jesus' resurrection in a new way this year? Spend time in prayer, thanking God for His gift of our Savior and Lord.

CLOSING

Congratulations, you finished this study! But this study isn't the end of the story. This study describes the completion of God's redeeming work through His Son . . . work that continues on through each of us.

Our prayer is that your study allowed you to sit at the feet of the Master Teacher as He passionately shared His last teaching moments with His disciples and the world. Through those moments, we pray that you've discovered something new about Jesus, thought about something differently, and come before Him in worship with renewed awe and confidence in what He has done for you. And we pray that you'll know more about Jesus tomorrow than you do today, and more the day after that, and the day after that, and . . . you get the picture.

So what's next? If you would like to study more about the life and ministry of Christ, consider these studies:

- **Christ**, our newly updated and revised study of the life and ministry of Jesus Christ through the gospels. This study leads you on a year-long venture that can deepen your understanding of and relationship with Jesus.
- **Jesus: Image of the Invisible** is a six-week study that reveals Jesus as the long-awaited Messiah and Savior of the world.
- **How to be Human** (for adults) or **Live It!** (for students) is a six-week study of Jesus' Sermon on the Mount that will challenge you to develop the traits that reflect God's character.

Whatever you choose to do next, we challenge you to continue studying. Continue praying. Continue learning. Continue growing. Continue the journey . . .

As the angel told the women who came to Jesus' empty tomb, "He is not here, for he has risen, as he said" (Mt. 28:6). May your celebration of the risen Christ become a time of renewed worship and a newfound desire to learn more about Him because you, too, have seen the Lord!

Christ the Lord is risen today. Hallelujah!

Margie Williamson
Editor

ABOUT THE AUTHORS

Roberta Watson has been married to Todd for more than thirty years, and they have two adult children. She has many wonderful memories of celebrating Easter with family and friends throughout her life. The celebration became more meaningful each year as her faith in Christ grew stronger and she had the opportunity to share that faith with her children.

Roberta began writing for Student Life Bible Study in 2004 while completing a Master of Arts in Christian Education at New Orleans Baptist Theological Seminary. She has served in the local church for more than twenty-five years as a Sunday School teacher, Women's Ministry leader, conference speaker, and association worker while continuing to work as a writer and editor with Life Bible Study.

Margie Williamson loves Easter. In fact, she accepted Christ as her Savior and Lord at the end of Sunday School on Easter morning, 1959, and was baptized that very evening. It was the first step in a long, growing relationship with Jesus Christ, that has impacted even her life's work. She married her college beau in 1974, and they've served in ministry ever since.

Margie has been writing devotionals and lesson materials since 1982, and has been working as an editor since 2007. She's discovered that both writing and editing lead to continued learning about God and His Word. Margie completed her undergraduate work at the University of Georgia, and her master's degree and her Ph.D. at the New Orleans Baptist Theological Seminary. Besides devotionals and lessons, she has written and published articles, poetry, textbook chapters, a training book of Youth Sunday School Workers, and a series of research articles in the Christian Education Journal. Her latest publication is a story she wrote about her mom in *Chicken Soup for the Soul: Best Mom Ever!*

ACKNOWLEDGMENTS

Publisher
John Herring

Design Editor
Margie Williamson

Editor
Roberta Watson

Graphic Design
Craig Robertson

Publishing Assistant
Bradley Isbell

Made in the USA
Middletown, DE
04 January 2021

30732439R00046